D1315624

start it

start it

New ideas for Sensational Appetizers

RUNNING PRESS
PHILADELPHIA · LONDON

A QUINTET BOOK

© 1999 by Quintet Publishing Limited

First published in the United States of America in 1999
by Running Press Book Publishers

Printed in China by Leefung-Asco Printers Ltd.

9 8 7 6 5 4 3 2 1

Digit on the right indicates the number of this printing

ISBN 0-7624-0503-1

Library of Congress
Cataloging-in-Publication Number 98-67645

This book was designed and produced by
Quintet Publishing Limited
6 Blundell Street
London N7 9BH

Creative Director: Rebecca Martin
Design: Deep Creative, London
Project Editor: Debbie Foy
Series Editor: Deborah Gray

Typeset in Great Britain by
Central Southern Typesetters, Eastbourne

This book may be ordered by mail from the publisher.
Please include $2.50 for postage and handling.
But try your bookstore first!

Running Press Book Publishers
125 South Twenty-second Street
Philadelphia, Pennsylvania 19103-4399

Material in this book has previously appeared in Quintet titles.

> **Because of the slight risk of salmonella, raw
> eggs should not be served to the very young,
> the ill or the elderly, or to pregnant women.**

contents

introduction

A starter should be a feast for the eyes and a flavorful fanfare for the main event to come. **start it** is brimful of exquisite dishes that will leave your guests breathless with anticipation, setting the tone for the meal and ensuring that it kicks off in style.

Avoid spending hours on meticulous preparation, with **start it's** range of straightforward recipes, complemented by clear, step-by-step instructions and tantalizing illustrations. No compromise has been made when it comes to taste, as all the dishes are tempting and imaginative, some traditional and some with a twist!

Ladle up an appetizing soup. Dressed up or down, served hot or cold, a dramatic bread and soup combo is always an impressive start to a meal. Or dip into dips, salsas, pâtés – a perfect recipe for a sociable first course. Savor a vegetarian starter to suit all palates, from classic Stuffed Peppers to the new and notable, with a range of global influences, such as Onion Chile Pie from the Caribbean.

Sample a fresh fish opener, from an exciting array of kabobs to the glamorous Lobster Gratin. Whatever you decide on, it is sure to go down a storm because **start it** works from three basic principles: fresh ingredients, simple preparation, and thoughtful seasoning.

With **start it** you'll always know where to begin...

dunk it

soups & breads

roasted pumpkin and smoked mussel soup

Ingredients

SERVES 6

1/2 SMALL PUMPKIN OR
1 MEDIUM FIRM-FLESHED
SQUASH (ABOUT 1 LB)

FRESHLY GROUND
BLACK PEPPER

3 TBSP OLIVE OIL

1 LEEK, SLICED FINELY

2 STICKS CELERY,
TRIMMED AND SLICED

1 CARROT, SLICED

2 TSP GROUND CORIANDER

3-4 SPRIGS FRESH THYME

1 BAY LEAF

1 3/4 PT WELL-FLAVORED
VEGETABLE STOCK

1 PT MILK

6 OZ SMOKED MUSSELS

SALT

PARSLEY, FRESHLY CHOPPED

Preheat oven to 425°F. Cut pumpkin into slices about 1½ to 2 inches wide and place them in a roasting pan. You will need six slices. Season lightly with pepper then brush flesh with olive oil. Bake in oven for about 30 minutes, until pumpkin is tender. Scoop flesh from skin and place to one side.

Heat 2 tablespoons of olive oil in a large pan; add leek, celery, and carrot and cook slowly until soft. Stir in ground coriander and cook slowly for a further minute. Add pumpkin flesh to pan with thyme and bay leaf, then pour in stock. Bring to a boil then cover and simmer for 35 to 40 minutes.

Allow soup to cool slightly then purée until smooth in a blender. Rinse pan then return soup to it with milk and bring slowly to simmering point. Add smoked mussels, season well with salt and pepper and heat for another minute or two. Garnish with chopped parsley just before serving.

beer mustard bread

Ingredients

MAKES 1 LOAF

1 PACKAGE (2¼ TSP) ACTIVE DRY YEAST

1½ TBSP SUGAR

1¼ CUPS WARM FLAT BEER, 105–115°F

3 TBSP POWDERED MILK

1½ TBSP VEGETABLE OIL

3 TBSP DIJON-STYLE MUSTARD

¾ TSP DRIED THYME

1½ TSP SALT

ABOUT 3 CUPS ALL-PURPOSE OR BREAD FLOUR

Dissolve active dry yeast and sugar in warm beer. Let yeast build up a foamy head, approximately 5 to 10 minutes.

Mix all remaining ingredients except flour. Put about 2½ cups flour into a large bowl and stir in oil mixture. When yeast is ready, stir it into flour. Turn dough out onto a floured surface. Knead with floured hands, adding flour as needed, for about 10 minutes, until you have a smooth dough that is neither sticky nor overly stiff. Place dough in a greased bowl and turn it over so all surfaces are lightly oiled. Loosely cover bowl and leave it in a warm place to rise until it has doubled in bulk, about 1½ hours.

Punch dough down and knead it lightly. Let it rest while you grease a 9-inch loaf pan. Gently shape dough into a loaf and put it in pan. Put pan in a warm place and loosely cover it. Let it rise until doubled in volume, about 1 hour. Twenty minutes before dough has finished rising, preheat oven to 350°F. Put loaf in oven and bake until golden, 25 to 30 minutes.

crisp breadsticks

Ingredients

MAKES **36 BREADSTICKS**

1 PACKAGE (2¹/4 TSP) ACTIVE DRY YEAST

1 TBSP SUGAR

1 CUP WARM WATER, 105–115°F

ABOUT **3 CUPS ALL-PURPOSE OR BREAD FLOUR**

6 TBSP VEGETABLE OIL

1¹/2 TSP SALT

ABOUT **3 TBSP VEGETABLE OIL**

1 EGG WHITE

2 TBSP WATER

SESAME OR POPPY SEEDS OR COARSE SALT, (OPTIONAL)

Dissolve active dry yeast and sugar in warm water. Let yeast build up a foamy head, approximately 5 to 10 minutes.

Put about 2¹/2 cups flour in a large bowl. Mix in 6 tablespoons oil and salt. When yeast is ready, stir it into flour. Turn dough out onto a floured surface. Knead with floured hands, adding flour as needed, for about 10 minutes, until you have a smooth dough that is neither sticky nor overly stiff. Place dough in a greased bowl and turn it over so all surfaces are lightly oiled. Loosely cover bowl and leave it in a warm place to rise until doubled in bulk, about 1¹/2 hours.

Grease two or three cookie sheets. When dough is ready, punch it down and knead lightly. Cut into 36 pieces. Roll each piece between your palms to form a very skinny rope, about eight inches long. Place breadsticks one inch apart on cookie sheets. Brush lightly with oil. Cover loosely and set in a warm place to rise, 20 to 25 minutes.

Preheat oven to 350°F. Make wash of egg white and 2 tablespoons water. Brush egg wash lightly over breadsticks. Sprinkle with seeds or salt, if desired. Bake until golden brown, about 25 minutes.

seafood chowder

Ingredients

SERVES 4

2 TBSP OLIVE OIL

2 LEEKS, SLICED

1 SMALL ONION, SLICED THINLY

1 CARROT, DICED

1 CELERY STALK, DICED

1 POTATO, DICED

2¹/₂ CUPS FISH STOCK

1 BOUQUET GARNI

1 LB COD FILLET, SKINNED

2¹/₂ CUPS MILK

8 SCALLOPS, SHELLED

³/₄ CUP QUICK-COOK MACARONI

SALT AND FRESHLY GROUND BLACK PEPPER

2 CUPS SHELLED, COOKED MUSSELS

2 CUPS PEELED, COOKED SHRIMP

4 TBSP PARSLEY, CHOPPED

FRESHLY GRATED PARMESAN CHEESE,

Heat oil in a large saucepan. Add leeks, onion, carrot, celery, and potato. Cook, stirring well, until leeks have reduced, and onion has softened slightly but not browned. Pour in stock and bring to a boil. Add bouquet garni, reduce heat, and cover pan. Simmer for 20 minutes.

Meanwhile, put cod in a saucepan, and add milk. Heat gently until milk is just about to simmer, then poach fish for 2 to 3 minutes, until just cooked. Remove fish from milk, and set it aside on a plate. Poach scallops in milk for 2 to 3 minutes, until just cooked. Set milk aside.

Flake cod, discarding any bones, and slice scallops. Add macaroni and salt and pepper to soup, and bring back to a boil. Then reduce heat, cover, and cook for about 7 minutes, or until macaroni is just tender. Pour in poaching milk, and heat, stirring all the time.

Taste soup for seasoning; then add cooked cod, scallops, mussels, and shrimp. Gently stir in parsley, and heat for 2 to 3 minutes, or until seafood is hot. Serve at once, with freshly grated Parmesan cheese.

tomato-basil soup

Ingredients

SERVES 4

2 CLOVES GARLIC, CHOPPED FINELY

5 TBSP FRESH BASIL, CHOPPED

1/4 TSP FRESHLY GROUND
BLACK PEPPER

3 TBSP EXTRA-VIRGIN OLIVE OIL

4 LB RIPE TOMATOES

1 CUP CHICKEN STOCK

1 TBSP BALSAMIC VINEGAR

1/2 TSP SALT

1/2 CUP SWEET RED PEPPER OR
TOMATO SALSA

In a small bowl, mix together garlic, 1 tablespoon basil, black pepper, and olive oil. Lightly crush garlic with the back of a spoon to release the juices into the oil. Let mixture steep while you prepare the tomatoes.

Peel tomatoes by dropping them into a pot of boiling water for about 40 seconds. Let them cool slightly, then slip off skins. Cut them in half and squeeze out seeds. Core and coarsely chop tomatoes.

Put tomatoes, chicken stock, and garlic-oil mixture into a medium saucepan. Bring to a boil, then reduce heat to low and simmer, uncovered, 1 hour. Add remaining basil, balsamic vinegar, and salt, then purée the soup. Taste and adjust seasonings. Chill until serving time. Top with a spoonful of sweet red pepper or tomato salsa, stirred into the soup.

bagels

Ingredients

MAKES 12 TO 15 BAGELS

1 PACKAGE (2¹/₄ TSP)
ACTIVE DRY YEAST

1 TBSP SUGAR

1 CUP WARM MILK, 105–115°F

3 CUPS ALL-PURPOSE
OR BREAD FLOUR

1 EGG

1¹/₂ TBSP VEGETABLE OIL

³/₄ TSP SALT

1 TBSP SUGAR

GLAZE

1 EGG WHITE

2 TSP WATER

SESAME OR POPPY SEEDS

Dissolve dry yeast and 1 tablespoon sugar in warm milk. Let yeast build up a foamy head, approximately 5 to 10 minutes.

Put about 2¹/₂ cups flour in a large bowl. Mix in egg, oil, and salt. When yeast is ready, stir it into flour. Turn dough out onto a floured surface. Knead, adding flour, for about 10 minutes, until you have a smooth dough that is neither sticky nor overly stiff. Place dough in a greased bowl and turn it over so all surfaces are lightly oiled. Loosely cover the bowl and leave it in a warm place to rise until doubled in bulk, about 1¹/₂ hours.

Punch down dough and cut into 12 to 15 pieces. Roll each piece between your palms to form a thin rope, about eight inches long with tapered ends. Bring ends together to form a neat circle, with tapered ends overlapping. With moistened fingers, pinch or lightly knead joined ends so the circle is securely fastened, or it will come apart later.

Set the bagels in a warm place to rise for 15 minutes and cover loosely. Preheat oven to 400°F. While they are rising, bring about 2 quarts of water to boil in a saucepan. Add 1 tablespoon sugar. Drop the bagels one or two at a time into boiling water, handling them as gently as possible so they do not deflate. They will rise to the surface of the water and swell up. Let them cook 1 minute, then turn and let them cook 3 minutes more.

Remove bagels, let drain over the water and place on a ungreased cookie sheet. Beat egg white with water and brush over bagels. Sprinkle with sesame or poppy seeds. Bake until golden, 20 to 25 minutes.

rye crescent rolls

Ingredients

MAKES **24 ROLLS**

**1 PACKAGE (2¼ TSP) ACTIVE
DRY YEAST**

1½ TBSP HONEY

1 CUP WARM FLAT BEER, 105–115°F

3 TBSP VEGETABLE OIL

1½ TSP SALT

1½ TSP CARAWAY SEEDS

1⅛ CUPS RYE FLOUR

**ABOUT 2¼ CUPS ALL-PURPOSE
OR BREAD FLOUR**

3 TBSP (⅓ STICK) MELTED BUTTER

Dissolve active dry yeast and honey in the warm beer. Let yeast build up a foamy head, approximately 5 to 10 minutes.

Mix oil, salt, caraway seeds, and rye flour. When yeast is ready, stir it into rye flour mixture. Stir in white flour, ½ cup at a time. When the dough becomes too tough to stir, turn it out onto a floured surface. Knead, adding flour, for about 10 minutes, until you have a smooth dough that is neither sticky nor overly stiff. Place dough in a greased bowl and turn over so all surfaces are lightly oiled. Loosely cover bowl and leave in a warm place to rise until doubled in bulk, about 1½ hours.

Punch dough down and cut into three equal parts. Let dough rest for 5 minutes. Oil two or three cookie sheets.

On a lightly floured surface, roll out first section of dough into a circle roughly nine inches in diameter. Cut circle into eight wedges. Starting from outside of circle and working toward the point, loosely roll up each wedge. Stretch each roll slightly and pull it into a curve. Set it on cookie sheet with point underneath. Repeat with all wedges, then with remaining dough.

Let dough rise until doubled, about 1 hour. Brush rolls with melted butter. Bake in a preheated 400°F oven until lightly browned, 12 to 15 minutes.

lebanese couscous soup

Ingredients

SERVES 6

4 LARGE ONIONS,
SLICED FINELY

3 CLOVES GARLIC,
SLICED FINELY

2 TBSP VEGETABLE OIL

1 TBSP (1/8 STICK) BUTTER

1 RED CHILE, SEEDED
AND CHOPPED FINELY

1 TSP MILD CHILI POWDER

1/2 TSP GROUND TURMERIC

1 TSP GROUND CORIANDER

SALT AND FRESHLY
GROUND BLACK PEPPER

41/4 PT WELL-FLAVORED
VEGETABLE OR CHICKEN STOCK

1/2 CUP COUSCOUS

FRESHLY CHOPPED CILANTRO,
TO GARNISH

Cook onions and garlic in the oil and butter until well browned, about 15 minutes, over a medium-high heat. Let onions brown to achieve a rich color for the finished soup.

Stir in chopped chile and spices and cook over a low heat for a further 1 to 2 minutes before adding stock. Season lightly then bring to a boil. Cover and simmer for 30 minutes.

Stir couscous into soup, return to boil, and simmer for a further 10 minutes. Season to taste then garnish with cilantro and serve immediately.

thai spiced chicken soup

Ingredients

SERVES 4

**1-2 TBSP PEANUT OR
SUNFLOWER OIL**

**2 SMALL, BONELESS CHICKEN
BREASTS, SKINNED AND
SHREDDED**

**2 TBSP THAI 7-SPICE
SEASONING**

**1 STICK LEMON GRASS,
CHOPPED FINELY**

2 MEDIUM POTATOES, DICED

**1½ PT CHICKEN OR
VEGETABLE STOCK**

1 PT MILK

**3-4 SCALLIONS, TRIMMED
AND SLICED FINELY**

²/₃ CUP FROZEN PEAS

**1-2 TBSP SATÉ SAUCE
OR PEANUT BUTTER**

**SALT AND FRESHLY GROUND
BLACK PEPPER**

**1-2 TBSP HEAVY CREAM,
TO GARNISH**

Heat oil in a large pan; add chicken and 7-spice seasoning and cook quickly until chicken begins to brown. Stir in lemon grass and potato, then add liquids. Bring slowly to a boil, then cover and simmer for 20 minutes.

Stir scallions into chowder with peas; return to a boil, then continue cooking for a further 5 minutes.

Add saté sauce or peanut butter to chowder just before serving. Remove from heat and stir until melted. Season to taste then serve, garnished with a spoonful of heavy cream.

crab and corn soup

Ingredients

SERVES 6

15-OZ CAN CREAMED CORN

8-OZ CAN WHITE CRABMEAT

**2¹/₂ PT WELL-FLAVORED
FISH, CHICKEN, OR
VEGETABLE STOCK**

**SALT AND FRESHLY GROUND
BLACK PEPPER**

1 TBSP SOY SAUCE

2 EGG WHITES (SEE NOTE, P.4)

FRESHLY CHOPPED SCALLIONS

Bring corn, crabmeat, stock, seasoning, and soy sauce to a boil in a large pan, stirring to mix corn and crab evenly throughout soup. Simmer for about 10 minutes.

Whisk egg whites into soft peaks, then stir carefully into soup just before serving. Garnish with a scattering of freshly chopped scallions.

dip it

dips, salsas, & pâtés

nut and cheese bell peppers

Ingredients

SERVES 4

1 CUP MIXED SHELLED NUTS
(PEANUTS, CASHEWS,
ALMONDS, ETC)

SALT

CAYENNE PEPPER

1 CUP LOW FAT CREAM CHEESE

1 CLOVE GARLIC, CHOPPED FINELY

FRESHLY GROUND BLACK PEPPER

1 MEDIUM RED BELL PEPPER

1 MEDIUM GREEN BELL PEPPER

WHOLE-WHEAT TOAST

Heat a skillet over a medium heat, then add nuts and cook until browned on all sides. Scatter some salt and cayenne over some paper towels, add hot nuts and toss in seasonings. Chop nuts roughly when cooled.

Beat cream cheese until smooth, then add garlic and nuts. Season to taste with extra salt and black pepper. Cut tops from peppers and remove seeds and cores. Pack filling into peppers, pressing down firmly with the back of a spoon until peppers are full.

Chill for 2 to 3 hours before slicing. Serve a slice each of red and green bell pepper, with whole-wheat toast.

mushroom and
hazelnut pâté

Ingredients

SERVES 6 TO 8

1³/₄ CUPS HAZELNUTS, TOASTED
AND CHOPPED ROUGHLY

1¹/₂ CUPS FRESH WHOLE-WHEAT
BREAD CRUMBS, TIGHTLY PACKED

1 MEDIUM ONION

2 PLUMP CLOVES GARLIC

1 LB MUSHROOMS, TRIMMED

4 TBSP (¹/₂ STICK) BUTTER

SALT AND FRESHLY
GROUND BLACK PEPPER

2 TBSP SOY SAUCE

1 LARGE EGG, BEATEN

2 THIN SLICES CANADIAN BACON
(OPTIONAL)

Preheat oven to 350°F. Combine hazelnuts with bread crumbs and chop onion, garlic, and mushrooms finely, preferably in a food processor.

Melt butter in a large skillet, add mushroom mixture, and sauté slowly for about 5 minutes. Allow to cool slightly, then add to hazelnut mixture with plenty of salt, pepper, and soy sauce. Blend together with the beaten egg.

Lightly grease a small loaf pan. Stretch bacon with the back of a knife, then arrange it in base of pan. Spoon the hazelnut mixture into pan and smooth top. Cover with greased aluminum foil and place in a shallow roasting pan. Half fill roasting pan with hot water.

Bake in preheated oven for 1 hour, then remove pâté from roasting pan and allow to cool. Chill pâté overnight in refrigerator, then loosen it in pan with a flat knife. Serve on a bed of green salad.

hummus

Ingredients

SERVES 8

³/₄ CUP GARBANZO BEANS,
SOAKED OVERNIGHT

2-3 PLUMP CLOVES GARLIC

¹/₃ CUP TAHINI (SESAME PASTE)

¹/₂ CUP OLIVE OIL

SALT AND FRESHLY
GROUND BLACK PEPPER

JUICE OF HALF A LEMON

PAPRIKA

Rinse garbanzo beans under cold running water, then bring to a boil in pan of fresh water and simmer for about 1¹/₂ hours, until tender. Leave to cool, then drain beans, reserving some of the water.

Place beans in a blender or food processor with garlic, tahini, and olive oil and blend. Add as much water from the beans as necessary to make a thick paste—about ²/₃ cup. Season well with salt and pepper, then add lemon juice to taste.

Spoon the hummus into a serving dish and chill lightly. Sprinkle with paprika just before serving.

traditional guacamole

Ingredients

SERVES 4

2 LARGE RIPE AVOCADOS

**2 TOMATOES, SEEDED
AND CHOPPED**

**1 MILD GREEN CHILE,
SEEDED AND CHOPPED FINELY**

**GRATED RIND AND JUICE
OF 1 LIME**

**2 SCALLIONS, TRIMMED
AND CHOPPED FINELY**

**1–2 GARLIC CLOVES,
CHOPPED FINELY**

¹/₂ TSP SALT

Scoop flesh from avocados and mash it roughly with a fork. Add all remaining ingredients, seasoning gradually with salt to taste. Serve with corn chips, tortilla chips, or a selection of sliced vegetables.

eggplant guacamole

Ingredients

SERVES 4 TO 6

1 LARGE EGGPLANT

1 AVOCADO, PEELED
AND CHOPPED FINELY

JUICE AND GRATED
RIND OF 1 LIME

2 TOMATOES, SEEDED
AND CHOPPED FINELY

1 GREEN CHILE, SEEDED
AND CHOPPED FINELY

1 TBSP ONION,
CHOPPED FINELY

1-2 GARLIC CLOVES,
CHOPPED FINELY

SALT AND FRESHLY
GROUND BLACK PEPPER

OLIVE OIL, TO DRIZZLE

PAPRIKA, TO TASTE

Preheat oven to 425°F. Prick eggplant all over, place on a cookie sheet, and roast for 30 to 40 minutes, until wrinkled and tender. Cover with a damp cloth and leave to cool completely, about 1 hour.

Peel eggplant, then chop into small pieces. Blend to a fairly smooth paste in a food processor, then turn into a small bowl. Toss avocado with lime juice and rind, then add to eggplant with next four ingredients. Stir carefully until well combined. Season generously with salt and pepper, then drizzle with a little olive oil and sprinkle with paprika.

Serve with tortilla chips or warm toast.

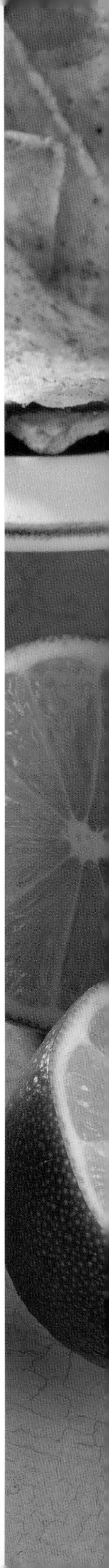

avocado salsa

Ingredients

MAKES ABOUT 2¹/2 CUPS

2 LARGE, RIPE AVOCADOS, PITTED AND DICED

3 TBSP FRESH LIME JUICE

1 TBSP OLIVE OIL

¹/3 CUP RED ONION, CHOPPED FINELY

¹/4 CUP RED BELL PEPPER, DICED

3 JALAPEÑO CHILES, CHOPPED FINELY

1 LARGE SEEDED AND CHOPPED TOMATO

1 TBSP FRESH CILANTRO, CHOPPED

2 GARLIC CLOVES, CHOPPED FINELY

SALT AND PEPPER, TO TASTE

Mix avocado chunks with lime juice and olive oil, then stir in remaining ingredients. Taste and adjust seasoning.

olive salsa

Ingredients

MAKES ABOUT 3 CUPS

**7-OZ CAN OF
PITTED GREEN OLIVES**

**3-OZ CAN OF
PITTED BLACK OLIVES**

**3 GARLIC CLOVES,
CHOPPED FINELY**

**2 JALAPEÑO CHILES,
CHOPPED FINELY**

**1/3 CUP RED ONION,
CHOPPED FINELY**

**1/3 CUP RED BELL PEPPER,
CHOPPED**

**2 OZ ANCHOVY FILLETS
(ABOUT 15), CHOPPED FINELY**

**1/4 CUP PINE NUTS, LIGHTLY
TOASTED**

2 TBSP OLIVE OIL

1 TBSP RED WINE VINEGAR

Drain olives and coarsely chop them. Mix with all remaining ingredients and let flavors blend for at least 30 minutes before serving.

To toast pine nuts: Preheat oven to 300°F. Spread pine nuts in a single layer on a small cookie sheet or a doubled sheet of aluminum foil. Bake for 5 to 10 minutes until they are lightly browned. Watch them closely, as they burn easily.

taramasalata

Ingredients

SERVES 4 TO 6

3 SLICES OF WHITE BREAD

4 OZ TARAMA (COD'S ROE USUALLY SOLD IN A JAR)

1 FRESHLY BOILED, TENDER, PEELED POTATO, LIGHTLY MASHED

1-2 GARLIC CLOVES, CHOPPED FINELY

1 SMALL ONION, CHOPPED

JUICE OF 2 LEMONS

3/4-1 CUP EXTRA-VIRGIN OLIVE OIL

2-3 SCALLIONS, SLICED THINLY

SEVERAL SPRIGS OF FRESH DILL, CHOPPED

BLACK OLIVES, TO GARNISH

Soak bread in cold water for 1 minute, then squeeze it dry.

Place tarama, soaked bread, potato, garlic, onion, and lemon juice in a blender, and beat until it forms a thick paste. Blend until smooth or slightly textured, as preferred.

Slowly add olive oil, a few tablespoons at a time, blending in between, until a thick, aromatic tarama-mayonnaise is formed. Taste and check for texture: if it is too strong, heavy, or dense, blend in a few tablespoons of water. Remove from blender and stir in scallions and chopped dill.

Spoon into a bowl and chill, then garnish with black olives and serve with fresh bread.

salmon pâté

Ingredients

SERVES 4

ONE **8-OZ** SALMON FILLET

$^1/_2$ CUP CREAM CHEESE

1 TBSP LIGHT SOY SAUCE

1 TBSP FRESH DILL, CHOPPED

1 TBSP FRESH PARSLEY,
CHOPPED

1 TBSP LEMON JUICE

1 TBSP CAPERS

GROUND BLACK PEPPER

$^1/_2$ TSP PAPRIKA

DILL SPRIGS AND LEMON
SLICES, TO GARNISH

HOT TOAST TRIANGLES

Poach salmon fillet in a large, shallow
pan for 8 to 10 minutes or until cooked
through. Remove from pan, drain, and
skin fish. Chop fish into pieces and
leave to cool completely.

Place cream cheese, soy sauce, dill,
parsley, lemon juice, capers, pepper,
and cooked salmon in a food
processor, and blend for 15 seconds.

Transfer to four individual ramekins
or small dishes. Sprinkle with paprika
and chill until required. Garnish with
dill and lemon, and serve with hot
toast triangles.

andalucian salsa

Ingredients

SERVES 4

1 LARGE CUCUMBER, DICED

3-5 SMALL, RIPE TOMATOES, DICED

1 CARROT, DICED

1 RED BELL PEPPER, DICED

1 GREEN BELL PEPPER, DICED
(ADD A YELLOW OR ORANGE BELL
PEPPER TOO, IF DESIRED)

3-5 SCALLIONS, SLICED THINLY,
OR 1 SMALL ONION, CHOPPED

3-5 GARLIC CLOVES,
CHOPPED FINELY

$1/4$ TSP GROUND CUMIN
OR CUMIN SEEDS

SALT, TO TASTE

JUICE OF 1 LEMON

1 TSP SHERRY VINEGAR
OR WHITE WINE VINEGAR

3 TBSP EXTRA-VIRGIN
OLIVE OIL OR TO TASTE

2 TBSP FRESH HERBS, CHOPPED
(PARSLEY, CILANTRO, MARJORAM
AND/OR OREGANO)

Combine cucumber, tomatoes, carrot, red and green bell peppers, scallions, and garlic. Toss with cumin, salt, lemon, sherry or white wine vinegar, olive oil, and herbs. Taste for seasoning, and chill until ready to eat. Serve with tortilla chips or fresh bread.

homemade tortilla chips

Ingredients

SERVES 4 TO 6

12 STALE TORTILLAS

1/3 CUP SALT (OPTIONAL)

VEGETABLE OIL FOR FRYING

To make chips, cut stale tortillas into strips or wedges. (If tortillas are fresh, dry them slightly by spreading them out and letting them sit for an hour or so.) For salted chips, make a brine by dissolving 1/3 cup salt in 2 cups water. Dip tortilla pieces into brine, then shake off excess water.

Pour 1/2 inch of vegetable oil into a large skillet and heat until oil is hot but not smoking. Add chips. If they are wet with brine, take care because oil will splatter. Cook chips until golden, turning once or twice, about 3 minutes, depending on heat of oil. Remove chips from oil, holding them briefly over pan to drain, then place them on paper towels. Give oil a few moments to reheat, then add a new batch of chips.

A fat-free alternative is to bake the chips. Preheat oven to 325°F. Spread prepared tortillas in a single layer on a ungreased cookie sheet. Bake, turning occasionally, until crisp and lightly browned, about 40 minutes.

black olive tapenade

Ingredients

MAKES ABOUT 1 CUP

¾ CUP PITTED BLACK OLIVES

¾ CUP PITTED KALAMATA,
NIÇOISE OR SPANISH
GREEN OLIVES

6 ANCHOVIES

1 GARLIC CLOVE

3 TBSP CAPERS

¼ CUP DRIED TOMATO
HALVES, PACKED IN OIL

¼ CUP FRESH BASIL, CHOPPED

1 TBSP FRESH THYME,
CHOPPED OR ¼ TSP DRIED

¼ TSP BLACK PEPPER

2 TSP FRESH LEMON JUICE

2-3 TBSP OLIVE OIL

Combine all ingredients in a blender
or food processor. Process until well
chopped, but stop before mixture
turns into a smooth paste. Add a little
extra olive oil if mixture is too dry.

savor it

vegetables

roasted tomato tartlets

Ingredients

SERVES 6

DOUGH

2 CUPS FINE WHOLE-
WHEAT FLOUR

$1/4$ CUP SESAME SEEDS

$1/2$ TSP SALT

1 LARGE EGG, BEATEN

5 TBSP OLIVE OIL

3-4 TBSP WATER

TOMATO FILLING

3 ONIONS, SLICED FINELY

2 GARLIC CLOVES, HALVED

3 TBSP FRUITY OLIVE OIL

3-4 SPRIGS FRESH THYME

2 BAY LEAVES

SALT AND FRESHLY
GROUND BLACK PEPPER

4-5 LARGE TOMATOES,
SLICED

Mix together flour, sesame seeds, and salt, then make a well in the center. Add egg and olive oil and mix to a soft dough, adding water as necessary. Divide mixture into six and shape to line six 4-inch individual tart dishes—this is more of a dough than a pastry and is easiest to mold into shape with your fingers. Chill tart shells for at least 30 minutes while preparing tartlet filling.

Cook onions and garlic in olive oil with thyme and bay leaves for 30 to 40 minutes, until well softened and reduced. Season to taste, then remove herbs from pan.

Preheat oven to 425°F. Fill tart shells with onion mixture then top with tomatoes, overlapping the slices and brushing them lightly with olive oil. Season well with salt and pepper, then bake in preheated oven for 20 to 25 minutes, until dough is crisp and tomatoes are just starting to blacken. Serve hot or cold with a crisp, green leaf salad on the side.

ntakos (cretan sandwich)

Ingredients

SERVES 4

4 PAXIMADIA OR OTHER WHOLE-WHEAT CRACKERS

12 OR MORE RIPE, SWEET, JUICY TOMATOES

SPRINKLE OF OREGANO

3 DOZEN BLACK GREEK OR OTHER MEDITERRANEAN OLIVES, PITTED AND CUT INTO PIECES

2 CUPS OR SO KEFALOTIRI OR PECORINO CHEESE, SLICED THINLY OR SHAVED

1/4-1/2 CUP OLIVE OIL (PREFERABLY GREEK), OR AS NEEDED

Arrange paximadia on a platter or on plates. Layer with tomatoes, oregano, olives, and cheese, and drizzle generously with olive oil.

Leave to marinate for at least 4 hours at room temperature, then serve.

eggplant toasts

Ingredients

SERVES 4

EGGPLANT PASTE

1/2 LB EGGPLANT, PEELED AND CHOPPED FINELY

1 EGG WHITE, LIGHTLY WHISKED

2 TSP SHERRY

2 TSP OYSTER SAUCE

PINCH OF GROUND GINGER

2 TSP CORNSTARCH

PINCH OF SALT

TOASTS

4 SLICES WHITE BREAD, CRUSTS REMOVED

VEGETABLE OIL FOR DEEP-FRYING

CHILES, SLICED THINLY, TO GARNISH

CUCUMBER, CHOPPED FINELY, TO GARNISH

Mix eggplant with remaining paste ingredients. Cut bread into bite-sized triangles, then spread on one side with eggplant paste.

Heat oil to 320°F in a wok, then carefully add triangles in batches with a spoon, paste side down, and fry for about 2 to 3 minutes, until bread is golden brown. Remove with a slotted spoon and drain on paper towels. Keep warm until all the toasts are cooked.

Serve warm, garnished with sliced chiles and finely chopped cucumber.

tortilla wheels with
pineapple salsa

Ingredients

SERVES 6 TO 8

FILLING

2/3 CUP CREAM CHEESE

1 GREEN CHILE, SEEDED
AND CHOPPED FINELY

2 TBSP CILANTRO,
FRESHLY CHOPPED

4 TOMATOES, SEEDED
AND CHOPPED FINELY

4 SCALLIONS,
CHOPPED FINELY

1 PEPPER, RED OR YELLOW,
SEEDED AND CHOPPED FINELY

1 CUP GRATED
CHEDDAR CHEESE

SALT AND FRESHLY
GROUND BLACK PEPPER

8 FLOUR TORTILLAS

SALSA

1 TBSP BLACK
MUSTARD SEEDS

1 ORANGE

4 THICK SLICES PINEAPPLE,
FRESH OR CANNED, CHOPPED

1 SMALL RED ONION,
CHOPPED FINELY

1 SMALL GREEN CHILE,
SEEDED AND CHOPPED FINELY

2 TOMATOES, DICED

Beat cream cheese until smooth, then add all other ingredients for filling. Mix well and season to taste with salt and pepper. Divide mixture between tortillas, spreading it evenly. Place each tortilla on top of another, making four stacks of two, then roll them up tightly. Cover in plastic wrap and chill for at least 2 hours.

Prepare salsa while tortilla rolls are chilling. Heat a nonstick skillet until evenly hot, then add mustard seeds and cook for 1 to 2 minutes, until the seeds begin to pop. Allow to cool. Grate rind from orange, then peel it and chop flesh. Mix orange with mustard seeds and all other ingredients, seasoning to taste with salt and pepper. Allow salsa to stand until required for flavors to blend.

Preheat oven to 400°F. Unwrap tortillas and trim away ends, then cut each roll into eight slices. Place on cookie sheets and bake in preheated oven for 15 to 20 minutes, until well browned. Serve with pineapple salsa.

crostini

Ingredients

MAKES ABOUT **40** PIECES

1 LARGE RED BELL PEPPER

2 BAGUETTES FRENCH BREAD, EACH CUT INTO ABOUT **20** SLICES

1 LARGE OR **2** SMALL TOMATOES, PEELED, SEEDED, AND CHOPPED

3 GARLIC CLOVES, CHOPPED FINELY

3-OZ CAN OF BLACK OLIVES, DRAINED AND CHOPPED COARSELY

1 JALAPEÑO CHILE, SEEDS INCLUDED, CHOPPED FINELY

ABOUT **8** ANCHOVY FILLETS, CHOPPED FINELY

2 TBSP FRESH BASIL, CHOPPED

¼ TSP DRIED OREGANO

2 TBSP OLIVE OIL

SALT, TO TASTE

10-12 OZ FRESH MOZZARELLA, SLICED THINLY

Preheat broiler. Rinse bell pepper, cut into four fairly flat pieces, and trim seeds and ribs. Place pieces under broiler, skin side up. Broil until skin is blistered and mostly black. Remove peppers from broiler and place in a covered bowl to steam for 10 minutes.

Put bread on broiler pan and broil, turning once, until golden on both sides. Meanwhile, peel and chop pepper. Put pepper in a bowl with tomatoes, garlic, olives, jalapeño, anchovy, basil, oregano, and olive oil. Mix ingredients. Taste and season if necessary. This salsa improves after flavors have been allowed to blend for several hours.

Spoon a little tomato mixture on each slice of bread, avoiding watery juices that will have collected in salsa. Top with a thin slice of mozzarella cheese. Broil until cheese has bubbled. Serve immediately.

pasta baskets with vegetables

Ingredients

SERVES 4

¼ LB DRIED VERMICELLI

DASH OF OLIVE OIL

VEGETABLE OIL, FOR DEEP-FRYING

FILLING

2 TBSP SESAME OIL

2 CLOVES OF GARLIC, CHOPPED FINELY

16 BABY CORN

¼ LB SNOW PEAS

2 CARROTS, SLICED THINLY

3 TBSP SOY SAUCE

1 TBSP TOASTED SESAME SEEDS

Bring a large saucepan of water to a boil, and add vermicelli with a dash of olive oil. Cook for about 5 minutes, stirring occasionally, until tender. Drain thoroughly and set aside.

Heat oil for deep frying, and pack one quarter of cooked vermicelli into a bird's nest, known as *nid d'oiseau*. (This is a small metal basket with long handles.) Otherwise, fry vermicelli in batches in a frying basket. Cook for 3 to 5 minutes in hot oil, until vermicelli is crisp and golden. Remove basket from bird's nest, and drain on paper towels. Repeat process to make three more baskets. Arrange baskets of loose vermicelli on individual serving plates. Set aside.

To make filling, heat sesame oil in a skillet and sauté garlic. Add corn, snow peas, and carrots, stir, and cook for 3 to 5 minutes, until tender. Stir in soy sauce and sprinkle with sesame seeds. Cook for a further 2 minutes, then spoon into vermicelli baskets to serve.

tomato and pasta timbales

Ingredients

SERVES 4

3/4 LB DRIED, MULTICOLORED
SPAGHETTINI

DASH OF OLIVE OIL,
PLUS EXTRA FOR GREASING

4 SMALL TOMATO SLICES

2 TBSP TOMATO PESTO

2 EGGS, BEATEN

1/4 CUP MILK

SALT AND FRESHLY
GROUND BLACK PEPPER

SAUCE

8-OZ CARTON SIEVED TOMATOES

1 TBSP SWEET SOY SAUCE

4 TBSP FRESH BASIL, CHOPPED

SALT AND FRESHLY
GROUND BLACK PEPPER

FRESH FLAT PARSLEY SPRIGS AND
CHERRY TOMATOES, TO GARNISH

Bring a large saucepan of water to a boil and add spaghettini with a dash
of olive oil. Cook for about 10 minutes, stirring occasionally, until tender.
Drain thoroughly and set aside to cool slightly.

Preheat oven to 325°F. Grease four individual ovenproof molds with a
little olive oil, and place a circle of waxed paper in the bottom of each.
Place a slice of tomato in base of each mold, then carefully pack in
spaghettini, leaving a 1/4-inch space at the top.

In a small bowl, combine tomato pesto, eggs, milk, salt, and pepper.
Beat well, then pour into each spaghettini mold, covering pasta. Arrange
molds in a roasting pan with enough boiling water to come halfway up
sides. Bake for 40 minutes, or until set and firm to touch.

Meanwhile, to make the sauce, place all the ingredients in a saucepan
and simmer, stirring, for 10 minutes, until thickened slightly.

Run a sharp knife around the edges of each timbale, then invert each on
to individual plates. Pour a little sauce around the base of each timbale,
and garnish with sprigs of parsley and cherry tomatoes.

stuffed peppers

Ingredients

SERVES 4

¹/₂ LB GNOCCHETTI SARDI
(SMALL DUMPLING SHAPES)

DASH OF OLIVE OIL

4 BELL PEPPERS, FOR STUFFING

FLAT LEAF PARSLEY SPRIGS,
TO GARNISH

FILLING

4 TBSP (¹/₂ STICK) BUTTER

6 SCALLIONS, CHOPPED FINELY

2 CLOVES OF GARLIC,
CHOPPED FINELY

1 BELL PEPPER, SEEDED
AND DICED FINELY

SALT AND FRESHLY GROUND
BLACK PEPPER

²/₃ CUP FRESHLY GRATED
PARMESAN CHEESE

Bring a large saucepan of water to a boil, and add gnocchetti sardi with a dash of olive oil. Cook for about 10 minutes, stirring occasionally, until tender. Drain thoroughly and set aside to cool slightly.

Preheat oven to 400°F. Lay each pepper on its side and slice off top, reserving it to make lid. Scoop out and discard seeds and pith. Arrange hollowed-out peppers in a shallow, ovenproof dish, and set aside.

To make filling, melt butter in a large skillet and sauté scallions and garlic for about 2 minutes, then add diced pepper. Season with salt and freshly ground black pepper and cook for about 5 minutes, stirring occasionally.

Add gnocchetti and the Parmesan cheese to filling mixture, and cook for about 2 minutes to heat through. Using a spoon, stuff each pepper with pasta filling, scattering any extra around the edges.

Place pepper lids in dish and bake for about 30 minutes, until peppers have softened. Just before serving, place in broiler for 2 to 3 minutes to char pepper skins, if desired. Serve garnished with parsley sprigs.

deep fried brie with salsa

Ingredients

SERVES 4

8 OZ FRENCH BRIE

1 EGG, BEATEN

2 CUPS FRESH WHITE BREAD CRUMBS

OIL FOR DEEP-FRYING

SALSA

1 TBSP SUNFLOWER OIL

1 SMALL ONION, CHOPPED FINELY

1 HUNGARIAN CHERRY PEPPER, SEEDED AND CHOPPED FINELY

1 RED FRESNO CHILE, SEEDED AND CHOPPED FINELY

1/2 CUP PRE-SOAKED APRICOTS, CHOPPED FINELY

2/3 CUP ORANGE JUICE

FRESH SALAD LEAVES, TO GARNISH

Cut Brie into four equal portions. Dip in beaten egg, then coat in bread crumbs. Cover lightly and place in refrigerator while preparing the salsa.

Heat sunflower oil in a pan and gently sauté onion, cherry pepper, and chile for 5 minutes. Add apricots and orange juice, and simmer for 15 minutes, or until the mixture reaches a chunky consistency.

Heat oil for deep-frying to 340°F and fry Brie for 3 to 4 minutes, or until golden. Drain on paper towels. Serve with apricot salsa, garnished with fresh salad leaves.

asparagus with bell pepper sauce

Ingredients

SERVES 4

3 RED BELL PEPPERS,
HALVED AND SEEDED

2 CUPS VEGETABLE STOCK

1 TSP CHILI SAUCE

JUICE OF 1 LEMON

1 GARLIC CLOVE,
CHOPPED FINELY

1 LB ASPARAGUS SPEARS,
TRIMMED

GRATED RIND OF 1 LEMON

PARSLEY SPRIGS, TO GARNISH

To make sauce, cook bell peppers under a hot broiler, skin side uppermost for 5 minutes until skin begins to blacken and blister. Transfer peppers to a covered bowl, seal and leave for about 10 minutes. Peel skin from bell peppers and discard.

Roughly chop bell peppers and put them in a saucepan with stock, chili sauce, lemon juice, and garlic. Cook over a gentle heat for 20 minutes or until peppers are tender. Transfer sauce to a food processor and blend for 10 seconds. Return purée to saucepan and heat through gently.

Meanwhile, tie asparagus spears into four equal bundles. Stand upright in a steamer or saucepan of boiling water and cook for 10 to 15 minutes until tender. Remove asparagus from pan and untie bundles. Arrange on four serving plates and spoon sauce over the top. Sprinkle with lemon rind, garnish with parsley, and serve.

tomato and heart
of palm slices

Ingredients

SERVES 4 TO 5

1 SQUARE WHITE SANDWICH LOAF

HEART OF PALM MAYONNAISE
AND CARROT MAYONNAISE

4 WHOLE EGGS

4 EGG YOLKS (SEE NOTE, P.4)

SALT

6 TBSP LIME JUICE

2-4 CUPS OLIVE OIL

1 LB CANNED HEART OF PALM,
WITH 5 TBSP LIQUID

2 CARROTS, CHOPPED AND COOKED

1 TSP GROUND BLACK PEPPER

2 TSP PREPARED MUSTARD

TOMATO FILLING

3 LARGE ONIONS, SLICED FINELY

3 GARLIC CLOVES, CHOPPED FINELY

6 TOMATOES, BLENDED

5 TBSP FRESHLY GRATED
PARMESAN CHEESE

2 TBSP ALL-PURPOSE FLOUR

SPINACH FILLING

1 LB SPINACH, CHOPPED FINELY

1 CUP MILK

SALT AND GROUND BLACK PEPPER

1 TBSP FLOUR

Put loaf in freezer for 30 minutes, so it will be easier to slice. Using a bread knife, slice bread into 1/2-inch horizontal slices. Then make piles of two or three slices and remove crust.

For heart of palm mayonnaise and carrot mayonnaise, put eggs, yolks, salt, and lime juice in a blender. In pulse mode, turn on and off for 5 seconds. Repeat. Turn on again and start pouring in olive oil, little by little. The mayonnaise will start to thicken.

When mayonnaise is ready, divide between two bowls. To one, add chopped heart of palm with reserved liquid. To the other, add chopped cooked carrots. Add half the pepper and mustard to each bowl.

For tomato filling, heat 3 tablespoons olive oil in a saucepan, and fry onions and garlic. When translucent, add blended tomatoes and Parmesan cheese. Cook for 10 minutes. Dissolve flour in a little water and pour onto tomatoes. This sauce should be thick, but remember it thickens when it cools. Adjust seasoning to taste.

For spinach filling, throw spinach into pan, pour in 1/2 cup of milk, and cook for 5 minutes. Add salt and pepper. Dissolve flour in remaining milk and then add to pan. Stir continuously until a cream consistency.

Now, place bottom slice of loaf on a rectangular plate and start to spread sauces over horizontal slices, alternating tomato, heart of palm, and spinach. Place top slice on top and, using a spatula, cover whole loaf with a generous layer of carrot mayonnaise.

Carefully insert some toothpicks through the layers and cover with plastic wrap. Chill for 1 hour before serving. Serve with green salad leaves.

onion chile pie

Ingredients

SERVES 6

9-INCH PIE CRUST

1¼ CUPS ALL-PURPOSE FLOUR

¼ TSP SALT

4 TBSP SOLID SHORTENING

4 TBSP (½ STICK)
CHILLED BUTTER

ABOUT 3 TBSP ICE WATER

FILLING

2 LARGE YELLOW ONIONS

2 TBSP BUTTER

2 POBLANO OR ANAHEIM
CHILES

2 CUPS GRATED MONTEREY
JACK CHEESE (ABOUT 8 OZ)

3 EGGS, LIGHTLY BEATEN

½ CUP SOUR CREAM

½ CUP MILK

¼ TSP GROUND CUMIN

¼ TSP WHITE PEPPER

½ TSP SALT

SLICED AVOCADO, TO GARNISH

To make crust, combine flour and salt. Using a pastry cutter or sharp knife, cut in shortening and butter until mixture has a coarse grain and tiny bits of shortening remaining. Sprinkle ice water over mixture, 1 tablespoon at a time, until dough forms a ball, that is not too sticky or overly stiff.

The dough will be easier to handle if you wrap the ball in plastic wrap and refrigerate it for 20 to 30 minutes. Roll out dough on a lightly floured surface to about 11 inches in diameter. Place dough in tart tin and unfold. Trim crust to a 1-inch overhang. Roll up overhang and pinch into a fluted edge. Refrigerate for 20 minutes before baking. Bake in a 400°F oven until slightly browned, 12 to 14 minutes.

For filling, slice onions, then cut slices in half and separate rings. Melt butter in a skillet. Add onions and sauté until golden brown, 20 to 25 minutes. While onions are cooking, prepare chiles. Roast chiles under a hot broiler until the skin is blistered and charred. Place in a bowl, covered with a towel, for 10 minutes to cool, then peel, seed, and chop.

Preheat oven to 350°F. When onions are ready, mix in chiles, then put onion-chile mixture in partially baked crust. Sprinkle grated cheese generously over onions.

Make a custard by combining remaining ingredients except avocado. Pour custard over the onions and cheese. Bake pie until custard is set and lightly brown, 40 to 45 minutes. Let it cool slightly, then serve warm, garnished with avocado.

selection of antipasti

braised artichokes

Ingredients

SERVES 4 TO 6

1/4 CUP PARSLEY, CHOPPED FINELY

2-3 TBSP FRESH MINT
LEAVES, CHOPPED FINELY

8-10 GARLIC CLOVES,
CHOPPED FINELY

SALT AND PEPPER, TO TASTE

1/2 CUP EXTRA-VIRGIN
OLIVE OIL

8 MEDIUM-SIZED ARTICHOKES

JUICE OF 1 LEMON

Combine parsley with mint, garlic, salt, and pepper, and about
3 tablespoons of olive oil, or enough to form a paste. Leave to marinate
and develop the flavors while you prepare artichokes.

Remove hard leaves from artichokes, and cut away sharp top from
tender, inner leaves. Pull center open, and scoop out thistly inside, using
a spoon and a sharp paring knife.

Stuff inside of each artichoke with herbed mixture, then lay artichokes in
a baking dish in a single layer. Sprinkle with salt, pepper, and any leftover
mixture, then with remaining olive oil and lemon juice, adding enough
water to cover artichokes. Cover with a lid or with aluminum foil.

Bake in a preheated 350°F oven for about an hour. Remove lid to taste
sauce; if it lacks flavor, pour into a saucepan and reduce until it
condenses and intensifies. Season with salt, pepper, and lemon juice,
then pour back over artichokes. Eat hot or cold.

roasted peppers in oil

Ingredients

SERVES 4

3 EACH: RED, YELLOW,
AND GREEN BELL PEPPERS

1 TBSP SALT

1/2 CUP WINE VINEGAR

1/2 CUP EXTRA-VIRGIN
OLIVE OIL

5 GARLIC CLOVES, CHOPPED

2 TSP PAPRIKA

1/2 TSP SUGAR, OR TO TASTE

Roast peppers by placing them on a
cookie sheet under a preheated broiler
for about 15 minutes on each side,
turning so that they char evenly.
Place in a covered bowl to steam for
about 10 minutes, then remove skins,
stems, and seeds.

Cut peppers into halves lengthwise,
and combine them with their roasting
juices, salt, vinegar, olive oil, garlic,
paprika, and sugar, as desired. Leave
to chill for at least 2 hours, or
overnight if possible, before serving.

italian-style marinated carrots

Ingredients

SERVES 4

8–10 MEDIUM-SIZED CARROTS

3–5 GARLIC CLOVES, CHOPPED

3 TBSP EXTRA-VIRGIN OLIVE OIL

2 TBSP RASPBERRY VINEGAR

3–5 TBSP PARSELY, CHOPPED

SALT AND PEPPER TO TASTE

Cut carrots into about ¼-inch thick slices. Steam or boil them until they are tender, about 15 minutes, Drain well, then toss with remaining ingredients and serve.

stuffed mushrooms

Ingredients

**MAKES 14 TO 16
MUSHROOMS**

3/4 LB LARGE MUSHROOMS

**1/4 CUP CRUMBLED
FETA CHEESE**

**1/4 CUP ITALIAN-STYLE
BREAD CRUMBS**

**1/2 TSP OLIVE OIL
(PLUS OIL FOR BRUSHING
THE MUSHROOMS)**

1 TSP LIGHT SOY SAUCE

1/2 TSP GROUND THYME

1 TSP GRATED ONION

3 TSP CAPERS, DRAINED

Wash mushrooms and remove stems.
Add 3 tablespoons of cheese,
together with bread crumbs, and mix
thoroughly. Stir in olive oil and soy
sauce. When well blended, stir in
thyme, grated onion, and capers.

Preheat broiler. Brush mushroom caps
with olive oil, inside and out. Stuff with
bread crumb mixture. Then crumble
remaining feta over mushrooms. Broil
until heated thoroughly, and tops have
begun to brown, about 6 to 8 minutes.

spanish salad of frisée

Ingredients

SERVES 4

**1 SMALL HEAD OF FRISÉE,
CLEANED AND CORED, CUT
INTO BITE-SIZED PIECES**

**2 ROASTED, RED BELL
PEPPERS, PEELED AND CUT
INTO STRIPS** (SEE P.50)

**3 OZ RIPE SPANISH CABRALES,
A BLUE CHEESE, CRUMBLED
(OR OTHER BLUE CHEESE
TYPE IF UNAVAILABLE)**

**10-15 PIMIENTO-STUFFED
GREEN OLIVES**

**3 TBSP EXTRA-VIRGIN
OLIVE OIL**

1 TBSP SHERRY VINEGAR

Arrange frisée, and garnish with roasted bell peppers, blue cheese, and green olives. Dress with olive oil and sherry vinegar.

pear gorgonzola salad

Ingredients

SERVES 4

1 HEAD ROMAINE LETTUCE, WASHED, SEPARATED, AND TRIMMED

2 PEARS

2 AVOCADOS

1/2 CUP CRUMBLED GORGONZOLA CHEESE

1/4 CUP SLIVERED ALMONDS

VINAIGRETTE OF YOUR CHOICE

Divide lettuce leaves among six plates. Cut unpeeled pears into thin lengthwise wedges, and core. Peel avocados and cut into thin lengthwise wedges. Alternate pear and avocado slices in sunburst arrangement on each plate. Sprinkle cheese and almonds over salad. Serve with vinaigrette on the side.

spring rolls

Ingredients

SERVES 4

3 TBSP PEANUT OIL,
PLUS EXTRA FOR BRUSHING

1 EGGPLANT, SLICED

1 SMALL ONION, SLICED FINELY

3 TBSP OYSTER SAUCE

1/2 CUP WATER

2 CUPS PREPARED
STIR-FRY VEGETABLES

SALT

8 SHEETS PHYLLO PASTRY,
MEASURING ABOUT **7** X **12** INCHES

SOY SAUCE

Heat oil in a pan, add eggplant and onion and cook gently until oil has
been absorbed. Mix oyster sauce with water, add to pan and continue to
cook slowly for about 10 minutes, until eggplant is tender. Remove from
heat and leave until cool enough to handle.

Preheat oven to 400°F and lightly oil a cookie sheet. Mix eggplant and
onion with stir-fry vegetables, adding a little salt if necessary. Fold phyllo
sheets in half and brush with oil to keep them moist. Divide vegetable
mixture between them and sprinkle each one with soy sauce.

Fold bottom and sides of the pastry in over filling, then roll pastry up into
a sausage, brushing edges with a little oil. Place on prepared cookie
sheet and brush lightly with oil again. Bake spring rolls in preheated oven
for 10 to 15 minutes, until pastry is browned and crisp. Serve immediately
with a rich soy sauce good for dipping.

chinese vegetable and omelet salad

Ingredients

SERVES 4

1 LB YOUNG CABBAGE

OIL FOR DEEP FRYING

1 TSP SALT

$1/2$ TSP GROUND CINNAMON

2 CUPS BEAN SPROUTS

4 SCALLIONS, HALVED LENGTHWISE

$1/4$ CUP CANNED WATER CHESTNUTS, DRAINED AND CHOPPED

1 RED BELL PEPPER, SLICED

1 YELLOW BELL PEPPER, SLICED

$1/4$ CUP SALTED CASHEW NUTS

OMELET

2 EGGS

$1/2$ TSP CHINESE 5-SPICE POWDER

DRESSING

2 TBSP LIGHT SOY SAUCE

1 TBSP LIME JUICE

1 TBSP SESAME OIL

$1/2$ TSP GROUND GINGER

Finely shred young cabbage. Heat oil in a wok and deep-fry cabbage for 4 to 5 minutes. Drain well on paper towels, and sprinkle with salt and cinnamon. Place in a large serving bowl. Top with bean sprouts, scallions, water chestnuts, peppers, and cashew nuts.

Beat eggs for omelet with Chinese 5-spice powder. Heat and oil a 6-inch omelet pan, then pour in eggs, tilting pan to coat base with egg. Cook for 2 minutes until top is set. Flip over and cook for 2 minutes more. Remove and cut into strips. Sprinkle over vegetables. Whisk dressing ingredients together, drizzle over salad, and serve.

sample it

fish & seafood

fish bites

Ingredients

SERVES 4

10 OZ COD OR SOLE, CUBED

2 TBSP LIGHT SOY SAUCE

1 TBSP LEMON JUICE

2 TBSP DRY WHITE WINE

1/2 TSP GROUND GINGER

1 LARGE ZUCCHINI

1 LARGE CARROT

1 TBSP FRESH DILL,
CHOPPED TO GARNISH

SAUCE

2/3 CUP DRY WHITE WINE

5 TBSP FISH STOCK

1 TBSP LIGHT SOY SAUCE

2 TBSP GINGER WINE

1 TSP FRESH GINGER,
CHOPPED FINELY

1 TBSP CORNSTARCH

2 SCALLIONS, CHOPPED

Place fish in a shallow dish. Mix soy sauce, lemon juice, white wine, and ginger. Pour over fish, cover, and marinate for 2 hours.

Meanwhile, using a vegetable peeler, slice zucchini and carrot lengthwise into thin strips. Blanch vegetables in boiling water for 1 minute, and then plunge them into cold water. Leave until cold. Soak four wooden skewers in cold water for 30 minutes so they do not char in cooking.

Remove fish from marinade, reserving liquid together with vegetable strips. Pat vegetables dry with paper towels. Wrap a piece of zucchini around each fish cube, and then a piece of carrot. Thread four cubes onto each wooden skewer, and brush them with marinade. Broil for 10 minutes, turning once, and rebrushing with marinade.

To make sauce, bring wine, stock, soy sauce, ginger wine, and ginger to a boil in a pan. Blend cornstarch with 2 tablespoons of cold water, and then add to pan. Return to a boil until thickened, add scallions and cook for 1 minute. Sprinkle with dill, and then serve with fish bites.

lobster gratin in pineapple shell

Ingredients

SERVES 4

1 LARGE PINEAPPLE

1 SMALL LOBSTER (16–20 oz)

SALT AND GROUND WHITE PEPPER

MIXED HERBS, TO TASTE

1/2 CUP DRY WHITE WINE

3 TBSP (1/3 STICK) BUTTER

4 SHALLOTS, CHOPPED FINELY

4 GARLIC CLOVES, CHOPPED FINELY

4 OZ MUSHROOMS

GENEROUS 1/2 CUP HEAVY CREAM

3 TBSP FRESH PARSLEY, CHOPPED

1 CHAYOTE, CUBED AND BOILED, OR 1 LB FRESH PEAS, COOKED

2 SMALL CARROTS, COOKED AND CUT INTO FINE 1/2-INCH STRIPS

A LITTLE GRATED PARMESAN CHEESE

Cut pineapple in half lengthwise, including through crown. Using a sharp knife, make a few cuts lengthwise to make it easy to remove flesh. Chop flesh and reserve. Place pineapple halves upside-down to drain.

Wash lobster. Tie some cooking string around them lengthwise, to fold tails inside. Put plenty of water in a large saucepan with some salt, mixed herbs, and wine. Bring to a boil and throw lobster in pan. Cook for 12 to 15 minutes, or until slightly reddish-pink.

Drain and let cool. Cut off string and, with kitchen scissors, make a cut into central part of belly. Scoop out meat, cutting it into chunks. Remove dark strip located along belly and discard.

Preheat a 375°F oven. Melt butter in a skillet and fry shallots. Add garlic, mushrooms, and salt and pepper. Reduce heat, add lobster and cream. Let cook for 5 minutes, taste for salt and pepper. Add parsley, chayote or peas, and carrots. Remove from heat and add pineapple pulp.

Pat pineapple skins dry and then fill with the mixture. Scatter a little Parmesan on top and bake in oven for 15 minutes until golden.

noodles with japanese fishcake

Ingredients

SERVES 4

2 SLICES JAPANESE FISH CAKE

1 CARROT

1 LEEK

4 OZ SNOW PEAS

$^1/_4$ HEAD BOK CHOY

12 OZ UDON NOODLES

SALT

$1^1/_4$ CUPS CHICKEN STOCK

12 LARGE, COOKED SHRIMP

DIPPING SAUCE

6 TBSP JAPANESE SOY SAUCE

2 TBSP SAKE

1 TSP SUGAR

$^2/_3$ CUP JAPANESE-STYLE STOCK

SMALL PINCH OF WASABI
(HOT HORSERADISH SAUCE)

1 SCALLION, CHOPPED FINELY

First prepare dipping sauce. Heat soy sauce, sake, sugar, and stock, stirring until sugar dissolves. Bring to a boil, then remove from heat, and let cool. Add wasabi, stir in scallion, then pour sauce into small dishes.

Now, prepare noodles, fish cake, and vegetables. Cut fish cake, carrot, and leek into matchstick-sized strips. Top and tail snow peas, and finely shred Bok Choy. Cook noodles in boiling salted water until tender. Meanwhile, bring chicken stock to a boil. Add carrot and leek, and simmer for 1 minute. Then add snow peas, and cook for a further minute. Finally, add Bok Choy, and bring back to a boil. Add shrimp, and remove pan from the heat. Leave to stand for 2 minutes.

Drain noodles, and divide them between four bowls. Carefully spoon vegetables and shrimp over noodles; then pour over stock. Top with pieces of fish cake, and serve immediately.

smoked salmon timbales

Ingredients

SERVES 4

TIMBALES

1 CUP SOUP PASTA

1 CUP RICOTTA CHEESE

1¹/₄ CUP SMOKED SALMON, CHOPPED

2 TBSP CHIVES, CHOPPED

1 TBSP PARSLEY, CHOPPED FINELY

1 LARGE EGG, BEATEN

GRATED RIND OF HALF A LEMON

SALT AND FRESHLY
GROUND BLACK PEPPER

SPINACH SAUCE

2 TBSP (¹/₄ STICK) BUTTER

1 SMALL ONION, CHOPPED FINELY

2 TBSP FLOUR

1¹/₄ CUPS MILK

8 OZ FRESH SPINACH
LEAVES, WASHED

FRESHLY GRATED NUTMEG

Preheat oven to 350°F. Base-line four individual soufflé dishes with non-stick baking parchment, and place on a cookie sheet.

Cook the soup pasta in boiling salted water until tender. Drain well. Mix pasta, ricotta, smoked salmon, chives, parsley, egg, lemon zest, and salt and pepper to taste. Spoon mixture into prepared dishes, pressing it down well. Cover with circles of non-stick baking parchment, and bake in preheated oven for 30 minutes, or until mixture has set.

Meanwhile, make spinach sauce. Melt butter in a saucepan. Add onion, and cook for 10 minutes, stirring, until softened. Stir in flour, then add milk, and bring to a boil, stirring. Add spinach, stir well, and cover pan. Simmer gently for 5 minutes, stirring occasionally. Purée sauce in a blender, then add salt, pepper, and nutmeg to taste. Rinse out pan, return sauce to pan, and reheat if necessary.

Pour some sauce onto warmed serving plates. Remove baking parchment from tops and slide a knife around the edge of timbales. Invert onto spinach sauce; then remove remaining baking parchment before serving.

stuffed mussels

Ingredients

SERVES 4

20 LARGE GREEN-LIPPED
MUSSELS, ON THE HALF SHELL

4 TBSP OLIVE OIL

1 LARGE ONION,
CHOPPED FINELY

1 RED CHILE, SEEDED
AND CHOPPED FINELY

1 SMALL EGGPLANT,
CHOPPED FINELY

2 GARLIC CLOVES,
CHOPPED FINELY

SALT AND FRESHLY
GROUND BLACK PEPPER

1 CUP FRESH WHOLE-WHEAT
BREAD CRUMBS

FRESH PARSLEY,
CHOPPED, TO GARNISH

Preheat oven to 425°F. Loosen
mussels on the half shells and arrange
them on a cookie sheet.

Heat oil in a large pan. Add onion and
chile and cook until starting to soften,
then add eggplant and garlic. Continue
cooking for 5 to 6 minutes, until all
vegetables are soft and lightly
browned. Season well, then add fresh
bread crumbs and mix thoroughly.

Pile a teaspoonful of filling into each
shell over the mussel, then bake in
hot oven for 12 to 15 minutes, until
piping hot. Serve immediately, with
chopped parsley to garnish.

tuna and eggplant kabobs

Ingredients

SERVES 4

20 OZ FRESH TUNA STEAK, CUT INTO 1-INCH CUBES

1 LONG, THIN, JAPANESE-STYLE EGGPLANT

MARINADE

GRATED RIND AND JUICE OF 1 LIME

1 TBSP OLIVE OIL

1 GARLIC CLOVE, CHOPPED FINELY

2 TBSP FRESH OREGANO AND PARSLEY, CHOPPED

SALT AND FRESHLY GROUND BLACK PEPPER

Place tuna in a non-metallic bowl, then add all marinade ingredients. Stir well and leave for at least 1 hour, stirring once or twice.

Half cook eggplant on barbecue or under broiler, until skin is just starting to wrinkle. Cut into 1/2-inch thick slices.

Soak kabob sticks in water to prevent them charring under broiler. Thread tuna and eggplant on skewers, then brush with remaining marinade.

Cook under a moderate heat for 5 to 6 minutes on each side, either on barbecue or under broiler, basting at intervals with any remaining marinade. Serve alone or with a rice salad.

crab and red pepper tartlets

Ingredients

SERVES 3 TO 4

4-5 TBSP (½ STICK) BUTTER

3 RED BELL PEPPERS, SEEDED AND CUT LENGTHWISE INTO THIN STRIPS

1 TBSP DILL, CHOPPED

4 SHEETS PHYLLO PASTRY, DEFROSTED IF FROZEN

½ CUP PARMESAN CHEESE, FRESHLY GRATED

8 OZ FRESH WHITE CRABMEAT

2 TBSP MAYONNAISE

1 TBSP LEMON OR LIME JUICE

In a large skillet over a medium heat, melt 2 tablespoons of butter. Add bell pepper strips and cook until softened. Remove from heat and stir in dill until thoroughly mixed.

Preheat oven to 350°F. Lightly grease eight 2½ x 1¼-inch muffin pan cups. Stack phyllo pastry on a work surface and cut into 4 to 5-inch squares.

Place one square on a work surface and brush lightly with a little butter; do not brush right up to the edge. Sprinkle with a little Parmesan. Place a second square on top of first at a right angle, to create a star shape. Brush lightly with butter and sprinkle with a little Parmesan. Top with a third square, at an angle to first two, but do not brush with butter. Ease into one of the muffin pan cups, keeping edges pointing up to form a flat-bottomed tulip shape. (Keep the phyllo pastry sheets you aren't working with covered with a damp cloth to prevent them from drying out.) Line remaining cups.

Bake until crisp and golden, about 10 minutes. Transfer to a wire rack to cool slightly. Carefully remove each phyllo case and set on a wire rack to cool. Divide pepper mixture evenly among tartlet cases and top each with a little crabmeat. Mix mayonnaise with lemon or lime juice and drizzle a little sauce over crabmeat. Garnish with miniature dill sprigs.

hawaiian coconut shrimp

Ingredients

SERVES 6

1¹/₂ LB JUMBO SHRIMP

2 TBSP HOISIN SAUCE

¹/₄ CUP FRESH LIME JUICE

1 TBSP FRESH GINGER, GRATED

1¹/₂ CUPS FLOUR

¹/₂ TSP SALT

2 EGGS

1 TBSP VEGETABLE OIL

1 CUP FLAT BEER

FLOUR FOR DIPPING, ABOUT ¹/₂ CUP

1¹/₂ CUPS COCONUT, SHREDDED

OIL FOR DEEP-FRYING

Shell and devein shrimp, leaving tails intact. Cut lengthwise through underside of shrimp so that top half opens up like butterfly wings. In a small bowl, combine Hoisin sauce, lime juice, and ginger. Put shrimp in a non-metallic bowl and toss with marinade. Cover and refrigerate at least 2 hours, stirring once or twice, to allow flavors to develop.

The batter also benefits from being made in advance. Combine flour and salt. In another bowl, lightly beat eggs with a fork, then add oil and beer. Stir liquid into flour until you have a slightly lumpy batter. Refrigerate batter until you are ready to cook shrimp.

Drain shrimp. Stir marinade into batter. Lay out ingredients in this order: shrimp, ¹/₂ cup flour in a small bowl, batter, coconut in a bowl, and a large, clean plate. Dip shrimp into flour and shake off any excess. Dip shrimp into batter and let excess drip off. Roll shrimp in coconut and pat on additional coconut if necessary. Put shrimp on plate.

Pour 3 inches of oil into a heavy pan and heat to about 365°F. Fry shrimp in batches until golden brown, about 1 minute. Drain and serve with a dipping sauce such as that on page 77.

mussels vinaigrette with walla walla sweets

Ingredients

SERVES 4

20-24 SMALL MUSSELS

1 CUP DRY WHITE WINE

1/2 CUP RED WINE VINEGAR

1 GARLIC CLOVE, CHOPPED FINELY

2 TSP DIJON-STYLE MUSTARD

2/3 CUP OLIVE OIL

1/4 TSP SALT

1/8 TSP PEPPER

2 TBSP FRESH PARSLEY, CHOPPED

1/2 LB YOUNG SPINACH LEAVES

4 SLICES OF WALLA WALLA SWEET ONION, SEPARATED INTO RINGS

1/3 CUP TOASTED HAZELNUTS, CHOPPED COARSELY

Scrub mussels with a brush to remove grit. Remove beards. Discard any mussels that do not close and put remaining mussels in a pot. Add wine and 1 cup water. Bring to a boil, cover and reduce heat. Simmer for 5 to 7 minutes until mussels open. Discard any that did not open. Put cooked mussels in a shallow, non-metallic dish.

While mussels are cooking, make vinaigrette. Combine red wine vinegar, garlic, mustard, olive oil, salt, pepper, and parsley. Whisk until well-blended. Pour over hot mussels. Cover and refrigerate for at least 6 hours, occasionally spooning marinade over mussels.

About 30 minutes before serving, remove mussels from refrigerator to return to room temperature. Divide spinach among four plates. Top with onion rings and hazelnuts. Divide mussels among the plates, spoon vinaigrette marinade over salads and serve.

pan-broiled
shrimp kabobs

Ingredients

SERVES **4**

8–12 MEDIUM TOMATOES

PINCH OF SUGAR

PINCH OF SALT

35–40 JUMBO SHRIMP,
IN THEIR SHELLS, HEADS
AND TAILS REMOVED
(OPTIONAL)

$^1/_3$–$^1/_2$ CUP EXTRA-VIRGIN
OLIVE OIL

2 TBSP BALSAMIC VINEGAR

3 GARLIC CLOVES, CHOPPED

SALT AND BLACK PEPPER,
TO TASTE

2–3 TBSP FRESH BASIL
LEAVES, TORN

LEMON WEDGES, TO SERVE

Preheat oven to 375°F. Place tomatoes in a roasting
pan, preferably a ceramic Mediterranean one, then bake
uncovered, for 20 to 30 minutes. The skin should have split,
exposing some flesh. Sprinkle with sugar and salt, then return
to oven and continue to roast for another 15 to 25 minutes.

Remove and let cool. It is best to let them sit overnight, as
the juices will run out and thicken. Remove skins of
tomatoes, and squeeze them to extract their flavorful juices.
Discard squeezed-out skins, and pour juices over roasted
tomatoes, then cut into halves or quarters.

Place shrimp in a non-metallic bowl for marinating; add
several tablespoons of olive oil, a teaspoon of balsamic
vinegar, and half the garlic. Leave for at least 30 minutes.
Soak eight to twelve bamboo skewers in cold water (or use
metal skewers to avoid soaking).Tightly thread shrimp onto
skewers. Save marinade to heat through as a pan sauce.

Heat a skillet and brown shrimp quickly on each side, for
only a few minutes, depending on their size. Remove to a
plate, and keep warm in a low oven.

Heat tomatoes in pan, then remove to plate, and sprinkle
with remaining garlic. Pour marinade into pan, heat through
until it bubbles, then pour over shrimp skewers and
tomatoes. Sprinkle with salt and pepper, then basil and serve
right away, accompanied by lemon wedges.

middle eastern swordfish kabobs

Ingredients

SERVES 4

2¹/₂ LB SWORDFISH

1 ONION, GRATED

8 GARLIC CLOVES, CHOPPED

JUICE OF 2 LEMONS

¹/₂ CUP EXTRA-VIRGIN OLIVE OIL

SEVERAL BAY LEAVES

SALT AND PEPPER

TAHINI SAUCE

³/₄ CUP TAHINI (SESAME PASTE)

2 GARLIC CLOVES, CHOPPED

FEW DASHES OF HOT-PEPPER SAUCE

FEW PINCHES OF CUMIN

SALT AND PEPPER

JUICE OF 1 LEMON

2 TBSP EXTRA-VIRGIN OLIVE OIL

¹/₂ CUP WATER, OR ENOUGH TO MAKE A SMOOTH, THICK SAUCE

FEW SPRIGS OF FRESH OREGANO

LEMON WEDGES, TO GARNISH

Combine fish, onion, garlic, lemon juice, olive oil, bay leaves, salt, and pepper. Marinate for at least an hour, preferably overnight in refrigerator.

Skewer marinated fish and bay leaves on either soaked bamboo (30 minutes in cold water) or metal skewers, alternating fish cubes with bay leaves. Though you don't eat bay leaves, they perfume the fish delightfully. Grill over a medium-low charcoal fire for about 8 minutes, turning to cook evenly, or broil under a preheated broiler.

Meanwhile, mix tahini with garlic, hot-pepper sauce, cumin, salt, pepper, lemon juice, and olive oil, then slowly stir in water until it reaches desired consistency. Taste for seasoning and adjust, if necessary.

Serve swordfish kabobs with sprigs of fresh oregano, accompanied by lemon wedges and a serving of tahini sauce on the side.

anticipate i

meat & poultry

thai lettuce parcels

Ingredients

SERVES 4

DIPPING SAUCE

2 TBSP THAI FISH SAUCE

2 GARLIC CLOVES, CHOPPED FINELY

1–2 TBSP SUGAR

2 TBSP LIME JUICE

2 TBSP WHITE WINE VINEGAR

1 BIRD'S EYE (THAI) CHILE,
SEEDED AND CHOPPED FINELY

PARCELS

1 TBSP CORN OR SUNFLOWER OIL

1 GARLIC CLOVE, CHOPPED FINELY

2 LEMON GRASS STALKS,
OUTER LEAVES REMOVED AND
CHOPPED FINELY

1-INCH PIECE FRESH GINGER,
PEELED AND CHOPPED FINELY

2–3 BIRD'S EYE (THAI) RED CHILES,
SEEDED AND CHOPPED

8 OZ CHICKEN BREAST, SKINNED
AND SLICED FINELY

1 TBSP SOY SAUCE

2 TSP THAI FISH SAUCE

4 OZ BEAN SPROUTS

1 SMALL ICEBERG LETTUCE, RINSED

Thoroughly mix all ingredients for dipping sauce together and leave for at least 30 minutes for flavors to develop and intensify.

Heat oil in a wok or large saucepan and stir-fry garlic, lemon grass, ginger, and chiles for 2 minutes. Add chicken and continue to stir-fry for 5 minutes, or until chicken is cooked. Add soy and fish sauce, stir once, then add bean sprouts and stir-fry for a further 30 seconds.

Arrange spoonfuls of chicken mixture on a lettuce leaf and drizzle with a little of the sauce. Roll up to form a parcel and serve.

eggplant and chicken strips

Ingredients

SERVES 4

SPICED FLOUR

1/2 CUP WHOLE-WHEAT FLOUR

2 TSP GROUND CINNAMON

2 TSP PAPRIKA

1 TSP SALT

STICKS

1 EGG WHITE

1 TBSP HEAVY CREAM

VEGETABLE OIL FOR DEEP-FRYING

1 LARGE EGGPLANT,
CUT INTO THIN STRIPS

2 LARGE CHICKEN BREASTS,
CUT INTO THIN STRIPS

3 TBSP SESAME SEEDS

SALT

LEMON WEDGES, TO SERVE

Mix flour with spices and salt in a shallow dish. Beat egg white with a fork until just frothy, then mix it with heavy cream.

Heat oil for frying to 375°F in a large pan. Dip eggplant and chicken strips in cream mixture, then turn them in spiced flour to coat well.

Deep-fry eggplant and chicken in batches until golden, then drain on paper towels. Scatter with sesame seeds and salt and serve with lemon wedges, and a serving of tartare sauce or mayonnaise.

potted ham with
eggplants

Ingredients

SERVES 4

2 LARGE EGGPLANTS

SALT AND FRESHLY
GROUND BLACK PEPPER

2/3 CUP MILK

1 TBSP (1/8 STICK) BUTTER

1 TBSP ALL-PURPOSE FLOUR

2 TSP DIJON OR
PEPPER MUSTARD

OLIVE OIL FOR FRYING
AND GREASING

4 TBSP DRY WHITE WINE

1 TSP POWDERED GELATIN

2/3 CUP COOKED HAM,
CHOPPED

2/3 CUP HEAVY CREAM

2 TBSP FRESH PARSLEY,
CHOPPED

Slice one eggplant very thinly. Lay slices on a cookie sheet in a single layer, sprinkle with salt, then leave for 30 minutes. Cook the other eggplant over a barbecue, under a broiler, or in a hot oven until skin is wrinkled and flesh is tender; turn once or twice during cooking. Cover with a damp cloth and leave for about 10 minutes, then peel off skin.

Heat milk, butter, and flour together in a pan until thickened and boiling, stirring all the time. Add mustard, salt and pepper, then remove from heat, cover with waxed paper to prevent a skin forming, and leave until cold.

Rinse salted eggplant thoroughly and pat dry on paper towels. Heat a little oil, then cook eggplant slices on both sides, a few at a time, until tender, adding more oil as necessary. Drain on paper towels and leave to cool.

Heat wine in a small pan until bubbling, then remove from heat and sprinkle on gelatin. Stir to dissolve, then leave for 2 to 3 minutes. Oil four individual bowls and line them with eggplant slices, overlapping them slightly around the sides.

Cut peeled eggplant into chunks, then purée it with ham in a blender or food processor. Whip cream until thick and floppy. Mix cream and ham mixture into sauce, blending well. Season with pepper; the ham should provide all the salt required. Stir gelatin again, then fold it into the ham cream with a generous half of the parsley.

Carefully spoon ham into prepared molds, banging them on worktop to shake mixture down. Chill for at least 2 hours before turning out the molds onto individual plates. Sprinkle with remaining parsley and serve with toast and salad.

sweet and sour
pork won tons

Ingredients

SERVES 4

ABOUT 6 OZ LEAN, BONELESS PORK

PINCH OF CHINESE 5-SPICE POWDER

1 TSP SESAME OIL

1 GARLIC CLOVE, CHOPPED FINELY

1 TBSP SOY SAUCE

18 SQUARES WON TON DOUGH OR READY-MADE WRAPPERS

1 EGG, BEATEN

OIL, FOR DEEP-FRYING

SWEET AND SOUR SAUCE, TO SERVE

Cut pork into small pieces, no bigger than $\frac{1}{2}$-inch cubes. Place the cubes of meat in a non-metallic bowl, and sprinkle with a good pinch of 5-spice powder, sesame oil, garlic, and soy sauce. Let marinate for a few hours, allowing time for meat to become well-flavored with garlic and spice.

Brush the middle of a square of won ton dough or a wrapper with a little egg, and place a piece of meat on it. Then gather dough around meat to make a tiny bundle with fluted edges. Fill and shape all the won tons in the same way. Then make Sweet and Sour sauce as given on page 77.

Heat sufficient oil to deep-fry won tons to 375°F, or until a cube of day-old bread browns in about 30 seconds. Fry won tons, a few at a time, until they have puffed up, are golden and cooked through. Drain well on paper towels. Serve immediately with Sweet and Sour sauce.

sweet and sour dipping sauce

Ingredients

SERVES 4

2 TBSP OIL

1 TSP SESAME OIL

1 LARGE ONION,
CHOPPED ROUGHLY

1 LARGE GREEN BELL PEPPER,
SEEDED AND DICED

1 LARGE CARROT, CUT INTO
MATCHSTICK STRIPS

6 TBSP TOMATO KETCHUP

$2/3$ CUP DRY SHERRY

2 TBSP SUGAR

4 TBSP CIDER VINEGAR

4 TBSP SOY SAUCE

8-OZ CAN PINEAPPLE
RINGS IN SYRUP

2 TSP CORNSTARCH

Heat both oils in a saucepan. Add onion, green bell pepper, and carrot. Stir-fry vegetables for 5 minutes, until they are lightly cooked, but still firm.

Stir in tomato ketchup, sherry, sugar, vinegar, and soy sauce. Drain pineapple, and mix a little syrup with cornstarch to make a smooth, thin paste. Add remaining syrup; then pour this mixture into sauce.

Bring to a boil, stirring all the time, then reduce heat, and simmer for 5 minutes. Cut pineapple rings into chunks, and add them to sauce. Remove from heat, and serve.

rich egg pasta dough

Ingredients

**MAKES A GENEROUS
$1^1/2$ LB PASTA**

4 CUPS WHITE BREAD FLOUR

1 TSP SALT

4-5 LARGE EGGS

Mix flour and salt in a bowl, making a well in the middle. Beat eggs, then pour two thirds into the well in flour.

Gradually mix in the flour, adding more egg until mixture clumps together. The dough may need 4 to 5 eggs to get the right consistency for a firm, manageable dough, depending on slight variations in absorbency of flour.

Mix and knead dough until smooth and pliable, and let sit before using.

kreplach

Ingredients

MAKES **72**

3/4 LB RICH EGG PASTA DOUGH

2 TBSP BEEF DRIPPING

1 SMALL ONION, GRATED

SALT AND FRESHLY
GROUND BLACK PEPPER

1¹/₂ CUPS GROUND,
LEAN ROAST BEEF

1 TBSP PARSLEY, CHOPPED FINELY

1 TBSP BEEF GRAVY

1 EGG, BEATEN

First, make rich egg pasta dough as given on page 77, and set it aside to rest while you make filling.

Melt dripping in a saucepan. Add onion, and cook, stirring, for 5 to 8 minutes, or until some of moisture has evaporated, and onion has lost its raw taste. Remove from heat, and stir in salt and pepper to taste. Then add beef, parsley, and gravy, which will bind mixture. Taste for seasoning.

Cut dough in half. Roll out one half to form a square slightly larger than 12 inches. Trim edges; then cut dough into 2-inch wide strips and across into 2-inch squares. Brush squares with beaten egg. Place a little filling in the middle of each square until you have used half of the mixture; then fold one corner of dough over to enclose filling, forming a triangular-shaped piece of pasta. Pinch edges of dough together well. Repeat with the remaining dough and filling to make sufficient quantity.

Cook Kreplach in boiling salted water, for about 3 minutes, until tender. Drain and serve with soup. Kreplach may also be served with a rich tomato sauce or gravy.

empanadas

Ingredients

SERVES 6

$^2/_3$ CUP GROUND PORK

$^2/_3$ CUP GROUND BEEF

1 SMALL ONION, CHOPPED FINELY

2 POBLANO, ANAHEIM CHILES, SEEDED AND CHOPPED FINELY

$^1/_2$ SMALL RED BELL PEPPER, SEEDED AND CHOPPED FINELY

$^1/_2$ SMALL GREEN BELL PEPPER, SEEDED AND CHOPPED FINELY

$^1/_2$ TSP GROUND CLOVES

1 TSP GROUND CINNAMON

1 TBSP TOMATO PASTE

5 TBSP WATER

1 TSP CLEAR HONEY

JUICE OF 1 LIME

$1^1/_2$ LB FROZEN SHORTCRUST PASTRY, DEFROSTED

OIL FOR DEEP-FRYING

Put pork and beef into a non-stick skillet and cook over a gentle heat, stirring constantly, for 8 minutes, or until meat has browned.

Add onion and chiles, and cook for 5 minutes, stirring frequently. Add both peppers and spices, and cook for a further 3 minutes. Blend tomato paste with water and add to pan, together with honey and lime juice. Bring to a boil, then simmer for 15 minutes, stirring frequently, or until most of liquid has evaporated. Allow to cool.

Roll pastry out on a lightly floured surface and cut out twelve 4-inch circles. Divide filling between pastry circles, brush edges with water and fold over to make small pastries. Pinch edges together firmly.

Heat oil to 350°F and fry Empanadas, a few at a time, for 3 minutes or until golden brown. Drain on paper towels and serve with a red or green chile sauce, green salad leaves and lime wedges.

index